T0099716

Thoughts from the Inside Out

A Journey of Self Discovery

Thoughts from the Inside Out

A Journey of Self Discovery

ADRIENNE LIRIO

Order this book online at www.trafford.com
or email orders@trafford.com

Most Trafford titles are also available at major online book retailers.

© Copyright 2010 Adrienne Lirio.
All rights reserved. No part of this publication may be reproduced, stored in a retrieval
system, or transmitted, in any form or by any means, electronic, mechanical, photocopying,
recording, or otherwise, without the written prior permission of the author.

Illustrators: Jason Parry & Carissa Galgano

Printed in the United States of America.

ISBN: 978-1-4269-4894-7 (sc)
ISBN: 978-1-4269-4895-4 (e)

Trafford rev. 11/15/2010

 www.trafford.com

North America & international
toll-free: 1 888 232 4444 (USA & Canada)
phone: 250 383 6864 ♦ fax: 812 355 4082

DEDICATIONS

Thanks to my loving sons Lloyd and Brandon for their encouragement to pursue my dreams in whatever form they may take. Their unconditional love and respect have been my greatest gift.

Thanks to my baby sister Lori who lets me sing whatever song I want just because I want to. Her loving indulgence of all my foibles and unwavering belief in me has always been my rock.

Thanks to Emily my muse whose righteous indignation against the world's slights inspired many of my favorite poems, and for her technical expertise.

Thanks to Stephanie who leant her wackiness and generous encouragement to the process.

Thanks to Jason who was willing to probe serious questions and provide his point of view. They were a great inspiration.

Thanks to Acacia for her honesty and encouragement.

And a special thanks to my parents Joan & Jay for providing me entrance into this world and for their love; along with the rest of my family and friends who knew I could do it.

"Thou shalt not be a victim.

Thou shalt not be a
perpetrator.

Above all, Thou shalt not be
a bystander."

-Holocaust Museum, Washington D.C.

TABLE OF CONTENTS

PROLOGUE

Having sat upon the razor's edge on many occasions for a variety of reasons feeling alone in my own misery I decided to be proactive about its relief.

I decided to write down my internal observations in the hopes it would bring insight and understanding. I chose to express these observations in two formats; poetry and what I call rant.

After sharing my own views with others it became all too clear that many of you are adrift in your own inner turmoil. I hope that I can help you understand that you are not alone in your confusion.

This book is intended as a journey of self-discovery and self-realization on an emotional level. Each of you will take from it something different. We all share a commonality in our human frailties and hopes although each of us experiences these things differently.

You may see yourself or someone close to you in these pages. Either way I hope you choose to garner some understanding from them. More importantly I hope that through this self-discovery you will choose to act upon these insights in order to seek your own betterment and happiness.

Remember that past is prologue and with each new understanding of that past you can create new and decidedly happier chapters in your life. You in your uniqueness are worthy of achieving a life filled with joy and love if you are willing to take a leap of faith and find your truth in this journey.

This work is not intended as a replacement for any professional help that may be required to alleviate more serious conditions such as clinical depression or bi polar disorder.

CHAPTER ONE

Why Regret?

WHY REGRET ?

What is depression? Well some might say that it is an extreme state of sadness, but it isn't! What it really is a deep chasm called REGRET.

Why Regret? Because whether it is the road not taken or perhaps the one that is there are outcomes and consequences to be dealt with. Some might even be real; at least they are to you.

In the scheme of things we aren't speaking of major or earth shattering events but seemingly inconsequential, small, quiet and to be sure insidious ones.

Each of these takes its toll on your confidence. Then it undermines the personal glue that allows you to keep your public mask in place.

With each assault you simply, slowly empty of everything you used to be. Your high expectations, hopes, minor accomplishments and even your optimistic views toward future successes all drip away in silence until there is nothing left but an empty shell. Hollow and bereft of anything meaningful you carry on.

If you are perseverant the shell maintains its routines and forward momentum, performing tasks without joy or relish but continues none the less. After all CONTROL is everything. It is not to be relinquished because then everyone will see the truth.

Why Regret? Because it's more than apparent that you are not young enough, self-absorbed enough or carelessly brainless enough. You are, however, too experienced, too caring, not to mention very unhappy.

Caught between necessity and misery you can only move forward without the spark that ignites the passion for what you do and who you are. It is a living death....

Why Regret? Because you had love and companionship and were inadequate to the task of keeping it. You lack the ability to make good decisions where the heart is concerned. No matter how fierce a friend or lover you are it is never quite reciprocated...this is beyond your comprehension and you are bewildered. Why are you so unworthy of this undeniable need? You do not know.

There is but one thing that can be held as truth without any regret and that is the love of your family. In this there is No regret!

Why Regret? Because you have spent a major portion of your life making competent decisions and directing others who look to you for guidance and support and find you are now paralyzed with indecision and inability. Now what is left for them to believe in? Now what do they see?

When life begs the question…What do you want to do now and where do I go from here? Where is the answer going to come from? It is disconcerting and disheartening when NO answer is forthcoming. What is life without purpose or direction? It is a road without any reason to be tread.

Why Regret? Because pride truly does go before a fall. To change things requires a return; in some respects, to the beginning. But it is so very far to go.

To start again in either direction or personality requires you to leave behind the ego that is the foundation holding up your perception of self.

But what is self? It is that which others perceive you as or that which you truly are. The true question here is do you even know who you are? Did you ever know? If you had perhaps you would have been more tenacious in pursuing what you desired.

It is the siren song of past desires lost or abandoned now; and the tortuous reminder that they are long gone and out of reach.

Some people are blessed with the ability to seek what they want and pursue it with an exclusionary abandon. Operating with a self-assuredness that they will succeed simply by virtue of wanting it they move forward. This requires a personality that insists on the universe bending to their wishes and miraculously it does! Practicality is just not a requirement.

Why regret? Because you are Not one of them. For you practicality and responsibility take precedence over personal desire. It requires you to put aside the fulfillment of your own selfish wants and provide what the universe demands. You do it because you know no other way.

Why Regret? Because memory, being what it is, is not truth but a recollection of past events and the people connected to them. It is fraught with feelings that both threaten and amaze but get mixed up over time.

These feelings and memories are like a placid lake serene and gentle until all at once they begin a waterfall slide over a deep precipice to somewhere deep and painful.

MOCK THE CLOCK

There are two groups of people
This world seems to see

The one for whom it's easy
And the other one with me

Although, I'm not alone here
My group is very small

A band of superheroes
Who refuse to take the fall

They insist on fighting always
For what they know is right

Though at times it seems so far
To see a win in sight

But they carry on responsibly
To battle every day

Completing everything that must be done
Without the thanks others rarely say

When all they want to do is scream
Till time itself stands still

They look at the mocking clock
And still they muddle through

They hope for some respite
From the never ending grind

But like all superheroes they
Pretend that they don't mind

GONE AWAY

Do you hear it?
    the silence
    the pain
    the dark
        my mind
                splintering
                    away

So many pieces
    they're sharp,
          relentless,
        attacking

Do you feel it?
    the quiet
    the emptiness
    the distance
        my soul
            slipping
              away

So many pieces
    they're hollow,
        transparent,
        haunting

Do you see it?
    the fear
    the loneliness
    the futility
        my life
            dying
                away

So many pieces
    they're agonizing,
        maddening,
      so fleeting

Away

THE DARK

Silence is both
Dark and deep

Especially when
Gone asleep

When the unrelenting
Black

Bites with razor
Sharp attack

Try to claw
Back towards the light

Don't be pulled
Down out of sight

The memories
They reach around

Screaming, wailing,
Pounding sound

It racks the brain
And shakes the soul

Rise with strength
And take control

Silence is both
Dark and deep

Until your fears
Again you meet

CHAPTER TWO

Why Me?

WHY ME?

Why Me? Have you ever raised your eyes skyward and said those words? Most of us have but; have you ever really stopped to think about it? Although, there are many things beyond your control there are a great deal that are not.

Why Me? You want to know why you are not chosen to belong to one group or another. Maybe you decry the lack of love or friendship. Perhaps you are angry for not securing the job you hoped for. You just can't understand what cosmic slight you have perpetrated to deserve such bad luck.

If you feel cheated by the cruelty of the universe for not getting what you wanted, wished for or coveted maybe it is time to reflect upon this injustice. Although, upon reflection a lack of confidence in yourself and your abilities or a lack of achievement could possibly be more accurate than any lack of luck.

Rejection, loss of acceptance or a blow to your self-esteem can lead to feelings of jealousy or envy. You may even go so far as to end up with a blinding case of hatred.

Why Me? Can it be that these emotions are a result of being victimized by others who consider themselves better some how or more worthy than you? Perhaps it is a group of people who choose to believe this nonsensical attitude is both right and appropriate. You know it isn't.

You know that it is emotional bullying and that it is as painful and detrimental as a physical beating. Worse yet you sometimes feel that these others are right about your unworthiness.

When you believe that it appears that circumstances bear out their considered opinion of your worth and your lack of skill you find it harder and harder to disagree with their negative assessment. It is harder still to climb out of that deep well of unhappiness you have crawled down into.

Why Me? Could it be you don't know who you are or what you have to offer? You think everyone must have something to offer. You're just not sure what you have. You consider what makes you unique and desirable as a friend, lover or employee. Still after much debate you remain unconvinced that you are of value. Where is the truth of it and why can't you take hold refusing to let anyone take it from you? Because, it is hard thing to accomplish. Self pity and self serving envy is so much easier.

Why Me? On the other hand; absolute, unwavering confidence in the fact that you are the better person to the detriment of all around you makes you an unlovable and unwanted aggressor.

No one loves or wants to be around a bully. Not even when you hide behind a passive-aggressive veneer of friendship. Confidence is good but are you using it as a club of obnoxious self righteousness?

In order to garner and maintain healthy interactions and relationships you must be willing to see the truth; not the perception of your own behavior and that of those around you.
Why Me? Because there is only one thing that you can truly control in your life and that is you. If you continue to insist that the universe is against you and that luck refuses to favor you and that generally everyone is out to get you without any ownership in your own lack of success than it will always remain just out of reach.

It is a sad fact that failure is easier than success. It is also a fact that bemoaning and whining about your failures is more widely accepted than to speak of ones accomplishments. Misery does truly love company and winning makes you a show off. What a backwards world it has become. Hard working is boring and obnoxious behavior equals cool.

JEALOUSY

All consuming fire

Cinders are all that is left

A heart blackened

ENVY

Envy it strangles love

Choking it like deathly vines

Cold and all alone

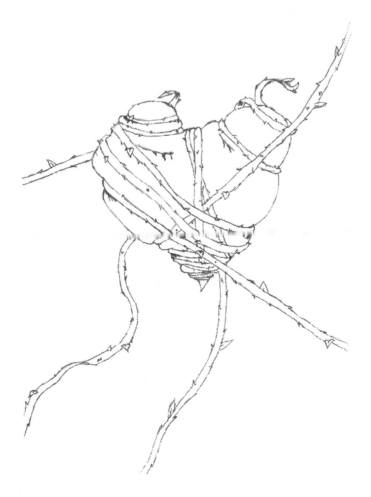

ALWAYS YOU

Always you
And never me

What are you
That I can't be?

What have you
Surely got?

That certainly
I have not

Each celebrates
His own gifts

Yet the choice
Again it shifts

Always you
And never me

What are you
That I can't be?

I keep trying
To compete

But the results
Just repeat

Could it be
Your golden face

Quiet nature,
Personality and grace

Capability and
Humor too

I really, really
Do hate you

My jealousy
Knows no bound

I hate you
Down to the ground

Why not?
When all I see

Is always you
And never me

JADE FIRE

Eyes that spark
In deepest green

Boiling inside
Shooting steam

Shaking with a
Violent rage

Monster breaking
From its cage

Spewing out
Without rein

Muscles clenching
Showing strain

Destructive power
Emerald hue

Erupts jade fire
Diminishing you

CHAPTER THREE

Why Anger?

WHY ANGER?

Why Anger? Because you have been told "you can't" or "you won't" attain your goals or your heart's desire so many times that you can only see red.

It is hurtful to think that others can dismiss you out of hand so easily that you can feel that perhaps they are right. Sometimes it makes it so much easier to give up and let your dreams fade than to stand up and fight for them.

Why Anger? Because when you feel that not going on and giving in to paralyzing defeat is NOT an option, anger becomes a great motivator.

Why Anger? Because when you refuse to fulfill the naysayers prophesies and prove the world wrong you will encourage your anger to wash over you and warm you against their cold predictions of failure.

Its heat fuels you and strengthens your resolve as you battle forth to fulfill your quest.

Anger turned inward however, can ravage a calm soul ripping it apart and leaving it damaged and spent.

Why Anger? Because it will slowly strip away your reserves and leave you in a state of constant turmoil without respite.

When your anger bubbles beneath the surface for too long without constructive outlet it can become a white hot flash of molten emotion that bursts forth leaving you to direct your anger in a detrimental way.

Although, you expect to feel great satisfaction once you've unleashed your anger at your target it sometimes just leaves you empty, disappointed and numb.

Why Anger? Because it's an easy response to cover up the way you feel. Perhaps, you feel trapped because you have done the wrong thing and can't or won't own up to it. You know you should do the right thing but instead you use righteous indignation to deflect what others think of you.

Why Anger? Because for all the energy it takes it has its place for both good or ill.

OH YEAH!

Sometimes I just need to win
Which means you simply don't

I could be the better one
But I think I simply won't

I know that truly in my heart
You're wrong and I am right

But you refuse to see the truth
Sometimes you're not too bright

Perhaps it's just denial that
Keeps the blinders on

The petty hurts and imagined slights
That come and are never gone

Maybe we could just this once
Pretend that we're mature

Well, I know that I sure can
But you I'm not so very sure

RISING

It starts as a bubble
That's barely there

It floats to the surface
Less and less rare

Starting out orange then
Crimson it glows

Then red rolling fire
It spreads and it flows

Now it's blue white
The brightest of flame

Looking for outlet
Release from the strain

Bursting out burning
All in its path

Cinders created from
Unbridled wrath

Creating and aiming
This deadly sin

Where is the target
Without or within

Confusion and pain
No matter which way

The heat will recede
The scars they will stay

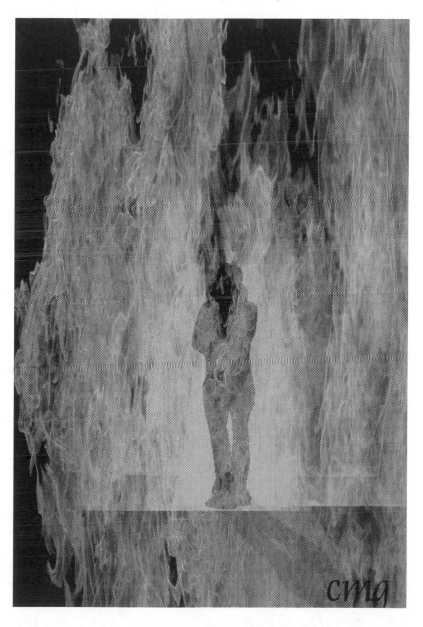

NOT ME

Anger, Anger flashing red
But do you stop to think

That no one said you must join in
Retreat back from the brink

Take a cool and cleansing breath
And then let your fury go

Others like to stir the pot
And watch the trouble grow

You could choose to stand alone
And check on what is true

Or open up your clueless mouth
Letting hurtful anger spew

Alliances have been torn
And friends you now destroy

I hope the devastation that you wrought
Has brought you endless joy

Go ahead and have your fun
I know you feel no shame

I feel I am quite the fool
Being sucked into your game

CHAPTER FOUR

Why Insensitivity?

WHY INSENSITIVITY?

Why Insensitivity? Because the universe is going deaf. The constant crying of the wronged, of the hungry and of those in pain is growing Louder and yet it's getting harder to hear.

The universe is also going blind. The ugly sight of racism, of violence and of War is getting uglier by the day. It is getting easier to look away and ignore it as though it weren't there.

Why Insensitivity? Because we look away and simply turn a blind eye and ignore it. It is too horrible to truly look at and too difficult to hear without going insane.

So we are cultivating an entire generation of people who are no longer attuned to hear or see the pain. It simply doesn't touch them.

Why Insensitivity? Because the daily individual dramas played out on every social network regarding both the mundane and the inane has become an acceptable substitute for dealing with the important issues of the day.

Why Insensitivity? Because there is no worldwide stage of serious problems to be addressed only the miniscule problems of the individual that are shouted out over the world wide web and demand immediate attention.

Have we become so completely self-absorbed that we truly cannot stop whining long enough to feel another persons pain or need above our own?

Why Insensitivity? Because we live in a keyboard generation where communication is a solitary experience without the benefit of personal interaction. This prevents real emotional understanding and a lack of communication skills.

Over time the interpersonal skills required for real communication and empathy for another has been lost.

FEED THE MONSTER

I cry out just a little
A small inconsequential sound

It sounds just like a whisper
As it falls deafly on the ground

I'm yelling a little louder now
A plaintive growing thing

But no one takes the time to hear
Certainly no solace does it bring

All I hear is screaming now
A wailing deep and shrill

Louder, growing louder, ever louder
Louder, LOUDER still

Why can't they hear me?
It's all my fault I dread

BECAUSE I CREATED THE MONSTER
DOESN'T MEAN I DON'T GET FED.

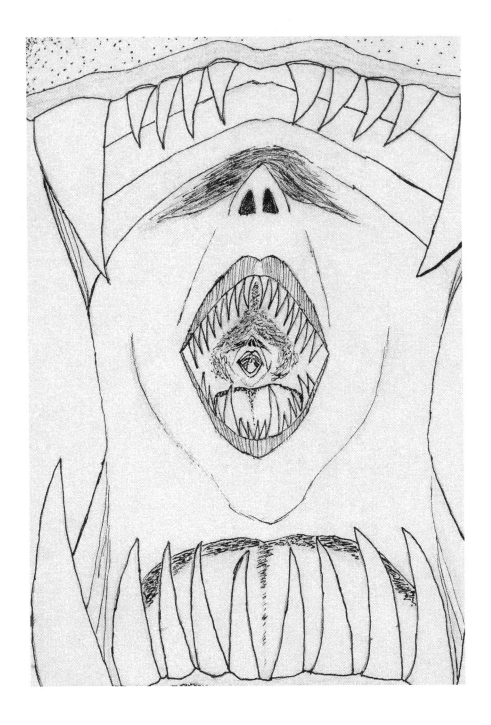

LONELY STAR

What must it be like
Always to be the center light

To have your unwavering glow
Incandescent and overly bright

Here in the universe
That silently spins

With you at the center
Always having to win

Everyone orbiting
Spinning around

As if your feet
Never had to touch ground

The stars in the heavens
Dare not interfere

When you are the center
Of all who can hear

It must be a burden
So heavy to bear

To always be right
In yourself without care

Adrienne Lirio

I envy you your assuredness
Radiating so clear

No wonder all others
Have to step to the rear

DRIPPING

Sticky condescension drips
From every pore

Continually dripping till
It pools upon the floor

Your false superiority is
Screaming in my ear

What do you see in me?
That causes you to fear

Perhaps it is
My calm disdain

That infuriates
Your sense of shame

For treating me
As you do

As if I'm from
Some lower zoo

Looking down
Your nose at me

Will gain you nothing
I can see

I shall not
Rise to your bait

But here and now
Will set you straight

Let your condescension drip
For I am here to stay

Unlike water against rock
I refuse to wear away

CHAPTER FIVE

Why Truth Or Perception?

WHY TRUTH OR PERCEPTION?

Why Truth? Some would say it is the absolute of what is and what has been. But it also includes that which we can perception. Right and wrong, memory and belief are not based on conventional truth but on your own need to hold onto what you require it to be.

Do you remember what you were like when you were younger? Are the memories pleasant, nostalgic, sad or perhaps unclear? What is it you remember most about your past? If you were asked to pick a time or incident that later defined you; could you? How about a specific person who was your greatest influence on you; who would that be? In remembering these things would the memory be truth or perception?

Why Truth? Because we all cling to our beliefs, sometimes too tenaciously, based on false premises. Some of your most important truths are based on nothing more than perceptive memory and the wish to make it so.

Why Truth? Because truth is different for everyone. No matter how many people share the same memory or experience they will never quite see it the same exact way.

There is to everything two truths the one being the absolute, unvarnished factual event and the other that which we choose to cling to as gospel fact.

With Truth, why do we need Perception? Because the world around us and our own desires and needs color what we choose to see and to believe. More importantly we choose how best to use it to fit our own universal view.

It is why we hold some memories close at hand while other we bury so deep as to render them non-existent. What is it that triggers these defenses? Is it fear or perhaps, if truth be told, we are somewhat embarrassed or ashamed of these memories. So we edit the uncomfortable details and remove altogether those we dare not acknowledge.

Why is truth so allusive and fleeting? Because it is in our own best interest to carefully edit our own back story. We fill in all the details that bolster the perception of who we want to be; especially in the eyes of others. We will be who we insist we are even if there is little truth in the reality of it. Like a well crafted play we take on our character like a costumed actor and we strive to play our part very well. Sometimes we are so accomplished at it we believe in it whole heartedly. After much time in that part you forget that is what it is.

The truth of you is no longer an option only the perception of you is available.

Why Perception? Because we cannot simply admit to our mistakes in poor judgment as a side affect of our humanity. Our petty cruelties, revenges and bouts of spoil sportsmanship, our lapses in human kindness and all that make us lesser human beings are painful failings we regret but cannot escape. Even though we all suffer from this uncomfortable truth we must perceive ourselves better than that.

Why Perception? Because we feel most deeply that these failings make us less than laudable as people. Our egos need acceptance and we cannot have the truth stand in way.

WHISPERS

Whispers
        Whispers
I can hear

Whispers
        Whispers
All too clear

Whispers
        Whispers
Telling lies

Whispers
        Whispers
Here truth dies

Whispers
        Whispers
What to choose

Whispers
        Whispers
What to lose

Whispers
Whispers
In your ear

Whispers
Whispers
Conscience clear

PERFECTION

You are so amazing-
You tell me everyday

Absolutely perfect
In oh, so many ways

For you it must
Be such a trial

To deal with others
Self denial

That you are all
That's truly great

What else more perfect
Could God create

In your heart
You know what's true

The sun and stars
Don't compare to you

I'm so grateful
That you're here

To show me perfection
I'll never near

In deference I could
Bow down low

Or simply bask
Within your glow

It is a most
Considered choice

But I must seek
A kinder voice

FOGGY

Seeing what you
Want to see

Truth obscured
By jealousy

Foggy senses;
False perception

Grabbing blindly
Poor deception

You insist it
Should be yours

Others say
They're not so sure

Believe what you
Want to be

Perception and truth
They don't agree

CHAPTER SIX

Why Loneliness?

WHY LONELINESS?

We have all, at one time or another, considered ourselves self-sufficient and completely without the need for anyone else's intervention. You would call that independence but I think its true nature is Loneliness.

Why Loneliness? Because for you self sufficiency is a requirement of survival. So you strike a pose of such commanding self reliance that your are to be envied and emulated by peers and subordinates alike. It is a shield that keeps everyone from knowing that what lies beneath the façade is a cold and empty place waiting to be touched by another.

Why Loneliness? Because in life there are leaders and followers. The leaders take charge of any and all situations. They radiate a disdain for those who cannot make a decision or do what is necessary.

You insist on competency in everyone but this is a fools paradise.

In the end your ability to get a positive result nets you praise and sometimes envy. You must by societies conventions with all possible humility accept their thanks and praise. You tell them it was nothing because after all you are so independent you require nothing from anyone.

But in the end when everyone has departed what is left? Only loneliness because accomplishment and competency do not warm you in the empty hours alone

Why Loneliness? Perhaps it is fear. Fear of hurt or fear of appearing weak. After all independent people are neither weak or vulnerable.

Weakness and vulnerability are distasteful and would create the outward appearance of need. The need for another's strength and support. How can you reach out for the support of another when you positively radiate your unwillingness to accept it.

Why Loneliness? Because each person who you have allowed to share your soul; as if it were a sweet, deep pool drank from it deeply but none too well. The slow poisoning of that precious place by detachment and abandonment has rendered it virtually undrinkable.

Why Loneliness? Because a fortress born of pain has walls so thick you are sure no one can breach them. Although, your most fervent wish is that someone will try.

What is the true nature of loneliness? Is it only a lack of companionship? You know that it is not as simple as being alone. There are times when you feel; more keenly; your loneliness when in the company of others.

You can participate with and appreciate the company of those surrounding you but the emptiness remains. Why? Deep down inside your heart you know why you can't fill the unending hollowness inside.

That empty feeling has been there for so long you can't honestly remember whether it was born of pain or loss. You hesitate to reach out because the consequences for failure are too great for your sense of self and your heart. So you don't take a chance and therefore, have already lost what might be because of what was.

Why Loneliness? Because loneliness creates all types of madness. You fear the very human need to connect to another in order to validate your existence. What happens If you remain without that validation? Are you a lesser person in the eyes of others? Perhaps just in your own eyes.

It doesn't happen all at once; but slowly you get the impression that others are looking through you. These intermittent disappearances then seem to become more frequent until you appear to disappear altogether.

So you walk like a ghost amongst the truly living.

WHERE IS YOUR HEART?

Where is your heart
When you need it?

Why has it ceased
to beat?

Who can say what
stops it

There must be a
reason you see

So we seek to
Find the answer

Why the silence
Continues on

For how long can
One continue

When love is
Seemingly gone

Where is your heart
When you need it?

Why has it ceased
To be?

Perhaps it hasn't
A reason

Without love between
You and me

JOURNEY

Alone I float upon the sea

The water rising, pitching me

Carried on the stormy waves

I ride from dawn toward my grave

Life's solitary journey done

Will I be missed by anyone?

WAITING

It seems so ironic

Finding only love platonic

To never find a heart that's true

That special someone just for you

Without a love to fill the space

The heart becomes a barren place

The emptiness you feel inside

No longer wants to be denied

What can you be waiting for?

Love to knock upon the door

It simply doesn't work that way

You need to come and join the fray

Or you could choose to stay apart

And you'll remain back at the start

No great love to fill you deep

What you sow, it's what you'll reap

CHAPTER SEVEN

Why Despair?

WHY DESPAIR?

Why Despair? Because no other feeling can so capture the absolute abandonment you feel. It is as if you exist alone for the sole purpose of swimming in inconsolable misery.

Is the cause of this state the effect that others have on you, experiences from your past or present or of your own creation; a self made, self imposed hell.

If you can create the hell; than surely you should be able to build the ladder with which to make your escape. Such a ladder could also be used to climb away from the darkness where others try to imprison you.

Why Despair? Because misery in itself can be like a dark cocoon in which to lose oneself. It's an excuse for removing yourself from feelings of joy, love, triumph and to stay out of the warmth of the light.

If you live in the dark long enough you have difficulty adjusting to the light. Your vision rebels and your thoughts shatter.

You could take a zealot's approach to a more positive outlook and choose not to give in to what is causing you this state of despair.

Why Despair? Because there are times when there is no balance between the dark and light. Sometimes your emotions seem to slip closer toward the dark side than to the light.

It can feel like an oppressive weight pressing you further and further away from the light; until you don't feel there's any lower you can go. When you finally reach your emotional rock bottom you can now look to turn your direction and perspective upward.

Remember, no one would ever know the pleasures of joy without experiencing its counterpart. To appreciate what is good we need to know the other side.

FREE FALL

SWIRLING

FALLING

SURGING

DOWN,
DOWN

TUMBLING

RUSHING

PLUMMETING

DROWNING

DOWN,
DOWN

SPIRALING OUT OF CONTROL
AT LAST THE BOTTOM

TOO LATE,
TOO LATE

CASCADE

They come unbidden for
Good reasons and faulty

They flow in waves hot,
Wet and salty

Solitary, shining,
Sliding on down

Sometimes there silent
And sometimes with sound

From under wet lashes
They constantly spill

Welling up, falling
Not stopping until

The cascade of tears
Ceases to flow

And you decide
To finally say no

Wet cheeks and chin
Are finally dry

You stop and move on
Till the next time you
Cry.

WHIRLWIND

The storm it circles
Whipped round

Drags your soul
From the ground

The tempest swirls
Around the eye

Where the calm
And silence lie

Reaching out from
Torments place

Ache to reach
That quiet space

Desperation mocks
Your try

As only anguish
Seems to fly

The swirling
Unrelenting storm

Of abject misery
It's born

Surrender to its'
Wretched spin

To abandon hope;
Despair must win

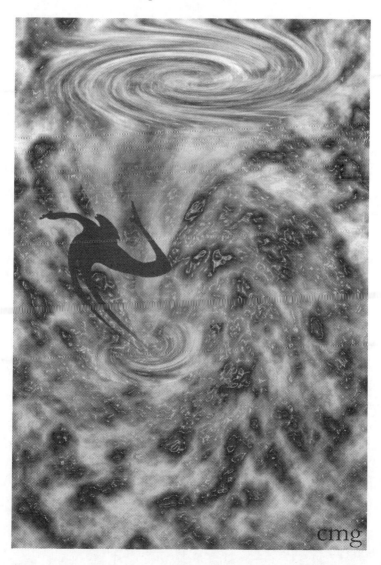

CHAPTER EIGHT

Questions For Your Thoughtful Contemplation

QUESTIONS FOR YOUR THOUGHTFUL CONTEMPLATION

1. Who do you most identify with in the poems? The victim or the aggressor?

2. Do you feel that you have always been the victim?

3. Has anyone ever pointed out that they are intimidated by you? If so; did you see their point of view or did you deny it?

4. How do you react when angered?

5. Do you do a slow burn or do you go off like a rocket?

6. Do you ever express yourself in a physical way?

7. Would you consider yourself a jealous person?

8. Is that the result of a personal experience?

9. What are you afraid of when it comes to relationships?

10. Do you find yourself envious of those around you?

11. What is it you envy?

12. Have you ever used your feelings of envy or jealousy as a motivator? If so how?

13. Have you ever used your emotions as an excuse or a crutch?

14. Have you ever lied to yourself to justify your own actions?

15. Did lying to yourself make you feel better about your self or worse?

16. Do you use lies to bolster your self-image or to garner a better place with a group?

17. How far will you take a lie?

18. Will you lie to hurt another?

19. Where have you encountered insensitivity?

20. Do you find greater insensitivity on the social networks due to distance and some anonymity?

21. Do you think people are more insensitive today due to a lack of communication skills?

22. Are people more insensitive due to constant desensitization from the world around them?

23. Do you think that the internet environment and desensitization encourages behavior like cyber-bullying, passive-aggressive communication,

constant drama and new social phenomenon like "frenemies"?

24. Do you feel the need to constantly share every moment of your day on a social network?

25. Do you love to be involved in other peoples' drama?

26. Do you constantly need to be the center of attention even if you have to create the drama to accomplish it?

27. Do you ever stop to consider what effect you have on others?

28. How do you react when your peers will not indulge your neediness?

29. Are you the person that is constantly called upon to mediate between the drama queens of the group? How do you like being in this position?

30. Have you ever been discouraged from following your dream based on someone else's perception of you? Did you accept their point of view or persevere in spite of it?

31. Are you lonely more often than not?

32. How do you handle loneliness?

33. Do you feel lonely even in the company of others?

34. Have you ever experienced true despair?

35. What is the difference between despair and drama?

36. What do you do to cope or escape from it?

37. Have you ever felt there was no coming back from despair? Why?

38. What have you done that you regret?

39. What haven't you done that you regret?

40. How do you cope with your regrets? In a negative or positive way?

41. Overall what did you take away from this journey?

42. Did you change your opinion or your view of yourself or others?

43. Have you been motivated to make changes in you life?

44. Is there anyone you now feel that you need to apologize to?

45. Is there anyone that you feel owes you an apology?

46. Do you intend to communicate your feelings regarding either the need to give or receive an apology?

47. Have you gained a better understanding of yourself and your motivations?

48. Do you now have some understanding that you are not unique or alone in your feelings?

49. Do you feel better equipped to open yourself up and see the other person's point of view?

50. Are you ready to continue this journey of self-discovery with a more positive outlook and an open mind?

THE ILLUSTRATORS

This book has had the pleasure of having two wonderful and extremely diverse illustrators. Their completely different styles add great dimension to the poetic journey and lend themselves to the often dark texture of the work.

JASON PARRY is the creator of Envy, Mock the Clock, Feed the Monster and Lonely Star.

Jason hand draws each illustration using pen and ink old school.

CARISSA GALGANO is the creator of the cover design, Journey, Rising, Waiting, Whispers, The Dark, Whirlwind and Cascade.

Carissa is from the new generation of computer artists and has her own design studio; Galgano Designs.

I gratefully acknowledge both these artists for their contribution to my work and hope they have added to your overall experience. Bravo to them both.

ABOUT THE AUTHOR

Adrienne currently resides in Branford, Connecticut. She has two grown sons; USAF Staff Sgt. Brandon Lirio and QC/QA chemist Lloyd Lirio.

Adrienne was an Assistant Professor for Quinnipiac University and extends her managerial expertise to various organizations while writing books and poetry.